TITANOSAUR

Life as the biggest dinosaur

TITAN

Life as the biggest dinosaur

First published by the Natural History Museum,
Cromwell Road, London SW7 5BD.

© The Trustees of the Natural History Museum, London,
2023.

A catalogue record for this book is available from
the British Library.

ISBN 978 0 565 09540 6

10 9 8 7 6 5 4 3 2

Story by David Mackintosh
Designed by David Mackintosh
All illustrations © David Mackintosh 2023.
www.profuselyillustrated.com

Reproduction by Saxon Digital Services

Printed by Toppan Leefung Printing Limited

Special thanks to Prof. Paul Barrett at the Natural
History Museum, London for checking the text.

OSAUR

Written & illustrated by David Mackintosh

Published by the

Natural History Museum, London

One morning,
Waterhouse was busy.
He was on the lookout
for something.
Something BIG.

Something VERY BIG.

Living at the Museum,
the little mouse thought
he had seen it all – *until
today.*

The place was buzzing
with exciting news of its
latest visitor.

It was called **TITANOSAUR**.

Scientists say Titanosaur
lived about 101 million
years ago.

It was not only the largest
dinosaur to have lived – it
was the biggest animal to
ever walk on Earth.

But
where was
Titanosaur
NOW?

It wasn't until 2014 that fossils
of the largest Titanosaur
were discovered on a ranch in
Patagonia, Argentina.

Waterhouse was astonished.

**"Why did it take so
long? Titanosaur is as
big as a house!".**

SI LO ENCUENTRA POR FAVOR REGRESE
AL RANCHO LA FLECHA, ARGENTINA.

Scientists named it

Patag
may

Even its NAME is big.

otitan orum

(**PAT**-a-go-tie-tan **MAYO**-rum).

The little mouse just had to see this!

He began searching *outside* the Museum.

'Where better to look for an animal the size of SEVEN male African elephants?'

Titanosaur was a herbivore, so Waterhouse knew to go straight to the Museum garden.

"The Museum garden is just a big salad to a Titanosaur."

This dinosaur was so big, it had to eat
129 kilogrammes of plants every day
just to produce enough energy to power its
enormous heart and lungs.

It could stand eating for hours, using its long
neck to reach leaves high on branches,
and down low for leafy shrubs.

The Titanosaur stripped the
leaves from trees using its rake-
like teeth, devouring all it could,
chomping its way through trees
and undergrowth.

And it would never have felt full!

Scientists say that this dinosaur wasn't choosy about the plants it ate. Its gut could digest even the toughest, spikiest plants.

The Museum garden was still in one piece – there was no sign that a fifty-seven tonne vegetarian had been there at all.

Waterhouse rested in the shade, puzzled that one enormous animal could be so difficult to find – *even with binoculars!*

Titanosaurs roamed the land in herds searching for leafy forests.

A herd made a lot of noise – the ground rumbled and the animals roared and cried out to one another across long distances.

It would be SO much simpler to find a whole herd of Titanosaurs!

Titanosaur

laid

thousands

of eggs

in its lifetime

so at least

a few

would survive.

It left the eggs

near volcanoes

so the warmth

would help them hatch.

But the dinosaur didn't watch over the eggs –
it was too busy looking for more food.

All this talk about food was making Waterhouse hungry.

Satisfied Titanosaur was nowhere to be seen outside the Museum (*let alone a herd of them!*) he decided to look *inside*.

It's quite a space – wide... tall... and definitely long.

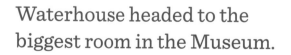
Waterhouse headed to the biggest room in the Museum.

The perfect place for a Titanosaur!

hiding.
be
could
it
where
building
in this
places
of other
plenty
were
there
then
If it wasn't in there,

Inside, he found the main hall empty – except for a Blue Whale and the usual crowds of fascinating human specimens.

Waterhouse's eagle eyes swept the space, watching for signs of the giant.

peg-like teeth...

scaly skin ...

eyes and nostrils up high on the head...

wide hips...

long neck and tail...

clawed hind feet...

And bad breath, probably.

But there was nothing here.

The little mouse kept searching.

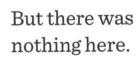

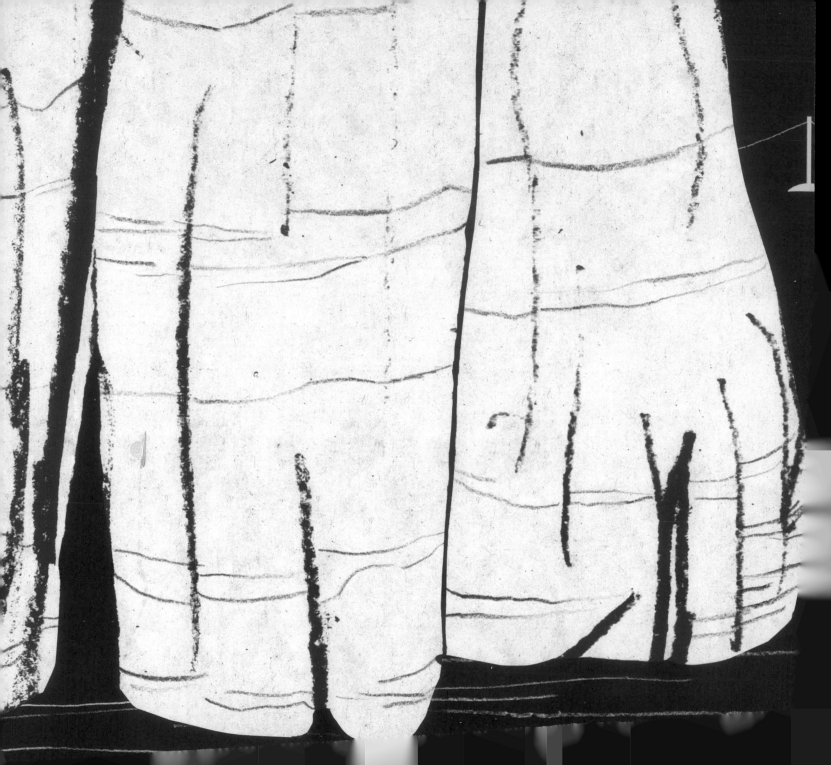

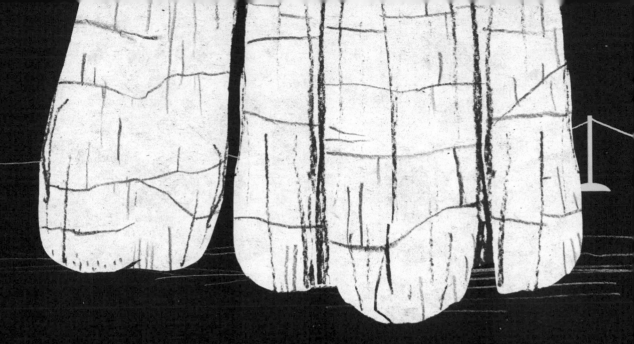

Titanosaur couldn't be upstairs –
the lifts only hold ten people which
isn't even the weight of one elephant.
It would need about 57 lifts to carry it.

Waterhouse sighed.

He had looked up and down, high and
low. He had been into every nook and
cranny, and searched the Museum
inside and out without even the
slightest hint of one single Titanosaur.

*Had he been on a wild-goose chase this
whole time?*

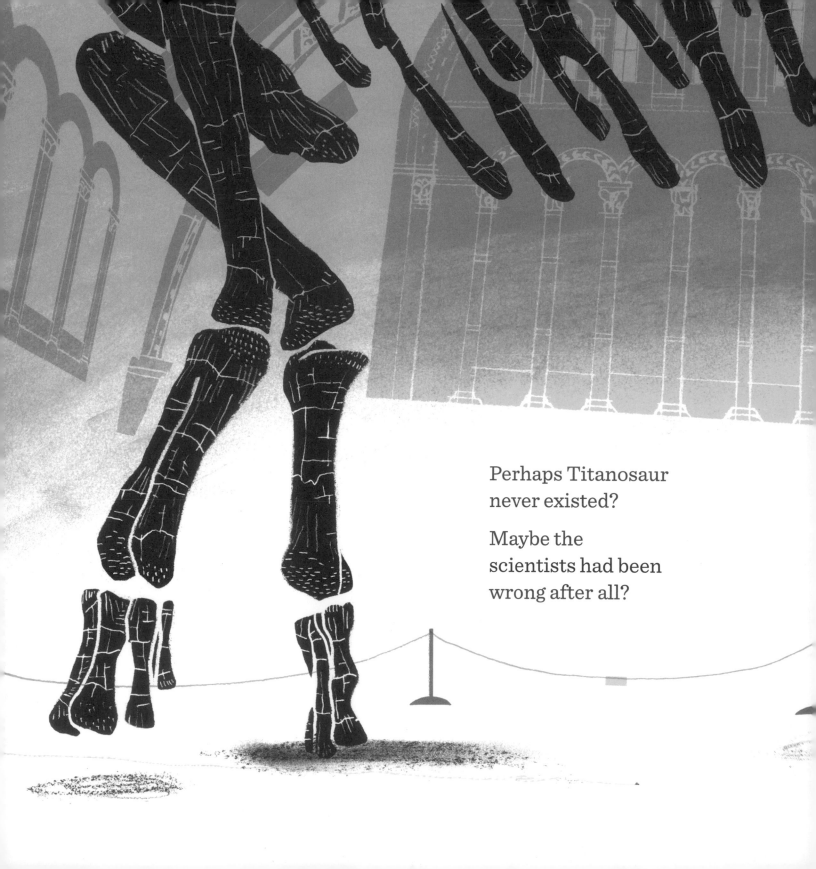

Perhaps Titanosaur never existed?

Maybe the scientists had been wrong after all?

PRIVATE:
no public
access

The Museum was now closed
and the visitors had gone.

Waterhouse's tiny legs were
tired – and his stomach growled
– so he returned to his home in
the wall. After searching all day,
there was no sign of Titanosaur.

But tomorrow was a new day.

That night, the little mouse had a
dream. And it was a BIG dream.